Informing the legislative debate since 1914

U.S.-Vietnam Relations in 2014: Current Issues and Implications for U.S. Policy

Mark E. Manyin
Specialist in Asian Affairs

June 24, 2014

Congressional Research Service

7-5700

www.crs.gov

R40208

Summary

After communist North Vietnam's victory over U.S.-backed South Vietnam in 1975, the United States and Vietnam had minimal relations until the mid-1990s. Since the establishment of diplomatic relations in 1995, overlapping security and economic interests have led the two sides to expand relations across a wide range of sectors. In 2013, President Obama and his Vietnamese counterpart announced a "comprehensive partnership" that is to provide a framework for moving the relationship to a "new phase." A key factor driving the two countries together is a shared concern about China's increased assertiveness in Southeast Asia, particularly in the South China Sea.

In 2014, the 113th Congress is likely to confront four inter-related issues with respect to U.S. relations with Vietnam: a 2014 bilateral nuclear energy cooperation agreement; Vietnam's participation with the United States in the 12-country Trans-Pacific Partnership (TPP) free trade agreement negotiations; questions about how the United States can influence human rights conditions inside Vietnam; and a debate over bilateral security ties, including whether to consider relaxing restrictions on military sales to Vietnam.

U.S. and Vietnamese Interests

In the United States, voices favoring improved relations have included those reflecting U.S. business interests in Vietnam's growing economy and U.S. strategic interests in expanding cooperation with a populous country—Vietnam has over 90 million people—that has an ambivalent relationship with China. Others argue that improvements in bilateral relations should be contingent upon Vietnam's authoritarian government improving its record on human rights. The population of more than 1 million Vietnamese Americans, as well as legacies of the Vietnam War, also drive continued U.S. interest.

Vietnamese leaders have sought to upgrade relations with the United States in part due to the desire for continued access to the U.S. market and to their worries about China's expanding influence in Southeast Asia. That said, Vietnam's relationship with China is its most important. Also, some Vietnamese officials remain suspicious that the United States' long-term goal is to erode the Vietnamese Communist Party's (VCP's) monopoly on power.

Economic Ties

The United States is Vietnam's largest export market and in some years its largest source of foreign direct investment. Bilateral trade in 2013 was almost $30 billion, a more than 60% increase since 2010. The United States and Vietnam are 2 of 12 countries negotiating the TPP. To go into effect, legislation to implement a TPP agreement (if one is reached) would require approval by both houses of Congress. Since the late 2000s, annual U.S. aid typically surpasses $100 million, much of it for health-related activities.

Human Rights

Human rights are perhaps the most contentious issue in the relationship. Although disagreements over Vietnam's human rights record have not prevented the two sides from improving relations, they appear to limit the pace and extent of these improvements. Vietnam is a one-party, authoritarian state ruled by the VCP, which appears to be following a strategy of informally permitting (though not necessarily legalizing) most forms of personal and religious expression while selectively repressing individuals and organizations that it deems a threat to the party's monopoly on power. Most human rights observers contend that for the past several years, the government has intensified its suppression of dissenters and protestors.

Some human rights advocates have argued that the United States should use Vietnam's participation in the TPP talks as leverage to pressure Hanoi to improve the country's human rights situation. Also, since the 107th Congress, various legislative attempts have been made to link the provision of U.S. aid, as well as arms sales, to Vietnam's human rights record.

U.S.-Vietnam Nuclear Energy Cooperation Agreement

In May 2014 the Obama transmitted to Congress a U.S.-Vietnam nuclear energy cooperation agreement, under which the United States could license the export of nuclear reactor and research information, material, and equipment to Vietnam. S.J.Res. 36, S.J.Res. 39, and H.J.Res. 116 would approve the agreement, which will enter into force upon the 90th day of continuous session after its submittal to Congress (a period of 30 plus 60 days of review) unless Congress enacts a Joint Resolution of disapproval.

Contents

Figures

Tables

Contacts

Developments in the First Half of 2014

South China Sea Tensions and Sino-Vietnam Relations[1]

In the late spring of 2014, longstanding tensions between Vietnam and China over competing territorial claims in the South China Sea flared, deepening U.S.-Vietnam cooperation on maritime security issues in Southeast Asia.[2] In early May, the state-owned China National Offshore Oil Corporation (CNOOC) moved a large exploratory oil rig into waters that Vietnam says lie on its continental shelf. The rig was positioned about 120 nautical miles from Vietnam's coast and less than 20 nautical miles from one of the Paracel Islands claimed by both China and Vietnam. Around 80 Chinese ships, including some Chinese coast guard and naval vessels, reportedly entered the area escorting the rig. Vietnamese patrol boats and fishing boats have entered the same waters, and a number of collisions between the Chinese and Vietnamese boats have occurred. Both sides blame the collisions on the other. China has said that the oil rig will remain in the area until August.

The U.S. State Department issued a statement describing China's deployment of the rig as a "provocative ... unilateral action" that "appears to be part of a broader pattern of Chinese behavior to advance its claims over disputed territory in a manner that undermines peace and stability in the region."[3] Assistant Secretary of State for East Asian and Pacific Affairs Danny Russel, speaking in June 2014, said that both China and Vietnam need to "exercise restraint," and that both "should remove all of their ships, and China should remove the oil rig.... "[4] The United States has not taken a position on specific territorial disputes in the South China Sea. Instead, the Obama Administration has focused on claimants' behavior.

Among legislative initiatives that touch on the South China Sea disputes, H.R. 4495, the Asia-Pacific Region Priority Act, states that U.S. policy urges all parties to the disputes to "refrain from engaging in destabilizing activities." S.Res. 167, which the Senate passed in July 2013, "condemns" maritime vessels' and aircrafts' use of coercion, threats, or force in the South China Sea and East China Sea to assert disputed maritime or territorial claims or alter the status quo. Among other items, S.Res. 167 "supports" U.S. military operations in the Western Pacific, including in partnership with other countries, to support the freedom of navigation.

As discussed in the "The South China Sea Dispute" section below, since 2010 the Administration has focused on encouraging all parties to negotiate a multilateral code of conduct and has criticized many of China's actions in the South China Sea for raising tensions in the region.

---

[1] For more on the South China Sea disputes, see CRS Report R42930, *Maritime Territorial Disputes in East Asia: Issues for Congress*, by Ben Dolven, Mark E. Manyin, and Shirley A. Kan; and CRS Report R42784, *Maritime Territorial and Exclusive Economic Zone (EEZ) Disputes Involving China: Issues for Congress*, by Ronald O'Rourke.

[2] China makes extensive claims, including marking on its maps an ambiguous "nine dash line" that covers most of the sea, including the Spratly and Paracel island groups. These claims overlap with those of Vietnam and three other Southeast Asian nations—Brunei, Malaysia, and the Philippines—which themselves have claims that conflict with each other. Taiwan also makes extensive claims mirroring those of the PRC. China, Taiwan, and Vietnam each claim the Paracel Island chain in the northern part of the sea. China controls them in practice, having forcibly taken control of the group in 1974 from South Vietnam.

[3] State Department Press Statement by Department Spokesperson Jen Psaki, "Vietnam/China: Chinese Oil Rig Operations Near the Paracel Islands," May 7, 2014.

[4] State Department, "Daniel Russel Regional Telephone Conference in Rangoon, Burma," June 10, 2014.

Negotiations between the Association of Southeast Asian Nations (ASEAN) and China over a Code of Conduct started in 2013, although rising tensions and divisions over what should be included in such a code have made progress difficult. China's actions in the South China Sea also have led the Obama Administration and the Vietnamese government to intensify collaboration in a number of security and maritime-related areas and fora. For instance, in December 2013 the United States said it would provide Vietnam with $18 million in assistance, including five fast patrol vessels, to enhance Vietnam's maritime security capacity. When asked during his confirmation hearing how to help foster a peaceful resolution to the South China Sea disputes, Ted Osius, the Obama Administration's nominee to be ambassador to Vietnam, said "I think we should explore further expansion of Vietnam's maritime domain awareness and how we can help Vietnam build its capacity to deal with the challenges in the South China Sea." He also said that it may be time to consider relaxing U.S. restrictions on the sale of military items to Vietnam.[5] For more on U.S.-Vietnam military-to-military relations, see the "Military-to-Military Ties" section below.

One reason many policymakers and observers were surprised by China's move to position the oil rig in disputed waters is that over the past two years, Hanoi and Beijing had expanded high-level ties and appeared to be committed to efforts to manage their maritime disputes. In 2011, the two countries signed an Agreement on Basic Principles Guiding the Settlement of Maritime Issues. Two years later, a 2013 bilateral agreement created working groups to discuss joint development in the disputed areas and a hotline to deal with fishery incidents. For Vietnam, maintaining stability and friendship with its northern neighbor is critical for economic development and security; Hanoi usually does not undertake large-scale diplomatic moves without first calculating Beijing's likely reaction. To date, even as it has protested the oil rig and China's cordon around it, Hanoi appears to be trying to avoid taking moves that could provoke Beijing, such as increasing its naval presence in the area, inviting U.S. Navy ships for unscheduled port visits, or initiating a legal case against China's actions and/or claims. For more background on Sino-Vietnamese relations, see the "Vietnam-China Relations" section below.

A factor influencing leaders in Hanoi is a significant anti-Chinese sentiment inside Vietnam. These emotions surfaced in the days after CNOOC's positioning of its oil rig. Protests involving thousands of Vietnamese ensued. Reportedly most occurred in urban areas, were peaceful, and appeared to be tolerated by Vietnamese authorities, who generally prevent large-scale gatherings. According to a *Wall Street Journal* investigation, Vietnamese human rights activists used the oil rig as an opportunity to organize the protests and many participants chanted slogans calling on the need for Vietnam to "change" in order to be "strong."[6]

Shortly after the peaceful protests occurred, Vietnam experienced its worst reported violent unrest in years in industrial areas on the outskirts of Ho Chi Minh City and in central Vietnam. Reportedly thousands of Vietnamese rioted, torching and creating large-scale damage at hundreds of foreign-owned factories. A number of individuals, perhaps including some Chinese nationals, appear to have been killed, though reports vary. According to several reports, most of the factories that were damaged were Taiwanese owned, though several of these employed many Chinese managers and laborers. Some Korean and Vietnamese factories also were damaged. According to

---

[5] CQ Congressional Transcripts, "Senate Foreign Relations Committee Holds Confirmation Hearing on Various Ambassadorial and U.S. Agency for International Development Nominations," June 17, 2014.

[6] Eva Dou and Richard C. Paddock, "Behind Vietnam's Anti-China Riots, a Tinderbox of Wider Grievances," *Wall Street Journal*, June 17, 2014.

some reports and analyses, the rioters appeared to be motivated at least in part by long-standing labor grievances. The aforementioned *Wall Street Journal* investigation reported that the rioters looted many of the targeted factories. In response, Vietnamese authorities reportedly arrested hundreds.[7]

Bilateral Nuclear Energy Agreement Signed[8]

U.S.-Vietnamese cooperation on nuclear energy and nonproliferation has grown in recent years along with closer bilateral economic, military, and diplomatic ties. In 2010, the two countries signed a Memorandum of Understanding that Obama Administration officials said would be a "stepping stone" to a bilateral nuclear cooperation agreement, under which the United States could license the export of nuclear reactor and research information, material, and equipment to Vietnam. In early May 2014, the two countries signed this agreement, and the Administration submitted it to Congress for review. Three bills have been introduced to date that would approve the agreement with Vietnam. Senate Foreign Relations Committee Chairman Robert Menendez introduced a resolution that would approve the agreement (S.J.Res. 36) on May 22. On June 9, 2014, Senator Majority Leader Harry Reid introduced S.J.Res. 39 and Representative Adam Kinzinger with Ranking Member of the House Foreign Affairs Committee Eliot Engel introduced H.J.Res. 116. Both of these bills provide for the approval of the U.S.-Vietnam nuclear cooperation agreement. The agreement will enter into force upon the 90th day of continuous session after its submittal to Congress (a period of 30 plus 60 days of review) unless Congress enacts a Joint Resolution of disapproval.

At least three issues are expected to be prominent if and when Congress takes up the agreement: (1) whether the agreement should have included stronger nonproliferation commitments, such as a legally binding commitment by Vietnam not to build uranium enrichment and reprocessing facilities; (2) the extent to which U.S. companies might benefit from an agreement; and (3) the extent to which Vietnam's human rights record and the growing U.S.-Vietnam strategic relationship should affect the decision to enter into a nuclear energy agreement.

In a move related to the bilateral nuclear energy agreement signing, in May 2014 Vietnam's government announced that it would participate in the multinational Proliferation Security Initiative (PSI), a U.S.-led group of about 100 countries that was established in 2003 to increase international cooperation in interdicting shipments of weapons of mass destruction (WMD), their delivery systems, and related materials.[9] In the past, Vietnamese officials said they would not join PSI because it operates outside the United Nations system.

---

[7] Patrick Boehler, "Just 14 factories targeted in Vietnam's anti-China protests belonged to mainland Chinese," *South China Morning Post*, updated May 20, 2014; Joshua Kurlantzick, "Vietnam Protests: More Than Just Anti-China Sentiment," *Asia Unbound* blog, http://blogs.cfr.org/asia, May 15, 2014; Dou and Paddock, "Behind Vietnam's Anti-China Riots."

[8] For more on this agreement, see CRS Report R43433, *U.S.-Vietnam Nuclear Cooperation Agreement: Issues for Congress*, by Mary Beth D. Nikitin, Mark Holt, and Mark E. Manyin.

[9] For more on the PSI, see CRS Report RL34327, *Proliferation Security Initiative (PSI)*, by Mary Beth D. Nikitin.

Introduction

Since 2002, overlapping strategic and economic interests have led the United States and Vietnam to improve relations across a wide spectrum of issues. Starting in 2010, the two countries accelerated this process, effectively forming a partnership on several fronts. Obama Administration officials identify Vietnam as one of the new partners they are cultivating as part of their "rebalancing" of U.S. priorities toward the Asia-Pacific, a move commonly referred to as the United States' "pivot" to the Pacific.[10] In 2010, the two countries mobilized a multinational response to China's perceived attempts to boost its claims to disputed waters and islands in the South China Sea, and they have continued to work closely on issues of maritime freedom and security. Additionally, the Obama Administration encouraged Vietnam to be a "full partner" in the ongoing 12-country Trans Pacific Partnership (TPP) free trade agreement negotiations and has given a higher priority to cleaning up sites contaminated by Agent Orange/dioxin used by U.S. troops during the Vietnam War. Over the past several years, the two sides also have signed a new agreement on civilian nuclear cooperation and have increased their non-proliferation cooperation. In 2013, President Obama and Vietnamese President Truong Tan Sang met in the White House and announced a bilateral "comprehensive partnership" that is to provide an "overarching framework" for moving the relationship to a "new phase." As discussed in detail below, the biggest obstacle to the two countries taking a dramatic step forward in their relationship is disagreements over Vietnam's human rights record.

U.S. Interests and Goals in the Bilateral Relationship

Currently, factors generating U.S. interest in the relationship include growing trade and investment flows, the population of more than 1 million Americans of Vietnamese descent, the legacy of the Vietnam War, the perception that Vietnam is becoming a "middle power" with commensurate influence in Southeast Asia, and shared concern over the rising strength of China. U.S. goals with respect to Vietnam include opening markets for U.S. trade and investment, furthering human rights and democracy within the country, countering China's increasing regional influence, cooperating to ensure freedom of navigation and operation in and around the South China Sea, and expanding U.S. influence in Southeast Asia. The array of policy instruments the United States employs in relations with Vietnam includes trade incentives and restrictions, foreign assistance, cooperation in international organizations, diplomatic pressures, educational outreach, and security cooperation. Since 2010, strategic concerns about China have taken on a larger role in the Obama Administration's formulation of U.S. policy toward Vietnam.

Vietnam's Interests and Goals in the Bilateral Relationship

For Vietnam's part, since the mid-1980s, Hanoi essentially has pursued a four-pronged national strategy: (1) prioritize economic development through market-oriented reforms; (2) pursue good relations with Southeast Asian neighbors that provide Vietnam with economic partners and diplomatic friends; and (3) deepen its relationship with China, while (4) simultaneously buttressing this by improving relations with the United States as a counterweight to Chinese

---

[10] For more, see CRS Report R42448, *Pivot to the Pacific? The Obama Administration's "Rebalancing" Toward Asia*, coordinated by Mark E. Manyin.

ambition.[11] By virtue of its economic importance and great power status, the United States has loomed large not only in Vietnam's strategic calculations, but also in domestic developments. For instance, Vietnam's protracted decision from 1999 to 2001 to sign and ratify the landmark bilateral trade agreement (BTA) with the United States—which Congress approved in October 2001—helped to break the logjam that had effectively paralyzed debate in Hanoi over the future direction and scope of economic reforms. Additionally, notwithstanding the legacies of the Vietnam War era, the Vietnamese public appears to hold positive views of the United States.[12]

There are a number of strategic and tactical reasons behind Vietnam's efforts to upgrade its relationship with the United States. Many Vietnamese policymakers seek to counter Chinese ambitions in Southeast Asia, and preserve its territorial and other interest in the South China Sea, by encouraging a sustained U.S. presence in the region. Vietnam also needs a favorable international economic environment—for which it sees U.S. support as critical—to enable the country's economy to continue to expand so it can achieve its goal of becoming an industrialized country by 2020. Securing greater access to the U.S. market, which already is the largest destination for Vietnam's export, would boost Vietnam's economy and is a major reason Vietnam is participating in the TPP negotiations.

A Ceiling on the Relationship?

Ultimately, the pace and extent of the improvement in bilateral relations is limited by several factors, including Hanoi's wariness of upsetting Beijing, U.S. scrutiny of Vietnam's human rights record, and Vietnamese conservatives' suspicions that the United States' long-term goal is to end the Vietnamese Communist Party's (VCP's) monopoly on power through a "peaceful evolution" strategy. However, it is possible that these concerns could be lessened, and the possibilities for strategic cooperation increased, if the United States and Vietnam both believe China is becoming unduly assertive in Southeast Asia.

Human Rights in the U.S.-Vietnam Relationship

As was true of their predecessors, Obama Administration officials have continuously expressed concerns—including via public criticisms—about human rights incidents.[13] Indeed, criticisms of Vietnam's human rights record appear to have played a significant role in convincing the Administration to oppose a number of items desired by Hanoi, such as expanding the types of arms that U.S. companies can sell to Vietnam. Concerns over human rights also appear to have been part of the reason the Administration chose not to hold a standalone summit meeting until

---

[11] Marvin Ott, "The Future of US-Vietnam Relations," Paper presented at The Future of Relations Between Vietnam and the United States, SAIS, Washington, DC, October 2-3, 2003.

[12] State Department Office of Research, *Vietnam: U.S. Image Gets a Boost*, Opinion Analysis, Washington, DC, September 9, 2008; and "Vietnamese Say U.S. Making Progress on Agent Orange," Opinion Analysis, Washington, DC, February 8, 2012.

[13] For instance, during a joint press appearance with Vietnamese Foreign Minister Pham Binh Minh in December 2013, Secretary of State John Kerry said, "... to realize our potential as a partner and for Vietnam to realize its potential as a thriving economy—and this is something we talked about openly and frankly—Vietnam needs to show a continued progress on human rights and freedoms, including the freedom of religion, the freedom of expression, and the freedom of association. I made this point clearly to Deputy Prime Minister Minh, as I have in all my previous discussions with Vietnamese officials." U.S. State Department, "John Kerry Joint Press Availability with Vietnamese Deputy Prime Minister and Foreign Minister Pham Binh Minh," Government Guest House, Hanoi, Vietnam, December 16, 2013.

July 2013. Likewise, Vietnamese leaders do not appear willing to fundamentally alter their treatment of dissenters or minority groups in order to more rapidly advance strategic relations with the United States.

However, differences over human rights have not prevented the two countries from improving relations overall, despite many signs that human rights conditions have deteriorated over the past few years. Barring a much more dramatic downturn in Vietnam's human rights situation, Administration officials appear to see Vietnam's human rights situation not as an impediment to short-term cooperation on various issues, but rather as a ceiling on what might be accomplished between the two countries, particularly over the long term.

Congress's Role

Throughout the process of normalizing relations with Vietnam, Congress has played a significant role. Not only has Congress advanced and designed bilateral initiatives, and provided oversight and guidance, but it also has shaped the bilateral interaction by imposing constraints and providing relevant funding, as well as through its approval process for agreements. Many Members have been at the forefront of efforts to highlight human rights conditions in Vietnam, as well as "legacy issues" of the Vietnam War, such as recovering the remains of missing U.S. troops and providing for the environmental remediation and the provision of health care services to areas contaminated by Agent Orange/dioxin used by the U.S. military during the Vietnam War. In the 1990s and early 2000s, many Members of Congress who favored improved bilateral relations provided the Clinton and George W. Bush Administrations with political backing for their policies of upgrading relations with Vietnam. Notably, these voices either have left Congress or appear to have become less vocal in recent years, coinciding with a rising perception that Vietnam's human rights situation has deteriorated. U.S. and Vietnamese participation in the TPP talks may provide Congress with another opportunity to exert influence over U.S.-Vietnam relations; Congress must approve implementing legislation if the TPP is to apply to the United States.

Sometime in 2014, Congress may also take up the U.S.-Vietnam nuclear energy cooperation agreement. However, the rules regarding consideration of such "123 agreements" reduce Congress' ability to use them to influence U.S. policy: the agreements enter into force upon the 90th day of continuous session after its submittal to Congress (a period of 30 plus 60 days of review) unless Congress enacts a Joint Resolution of disapproval. Even if both chambers of Congress pass such a resolution, it is subject to a Presidential veto.

Brief History of the Normalization of U.S.-Vietnam Relations

The United States' post-World War II military involvement in Vietnam began in the early 1960s, with the dispatch of military advisers to assist the South Vietnamese government (officially known as the Republic of Vietnam) in its battles with communist North Vietnam and indigenous (i.e., South Vietnamese) communist forces and their allies. Thereafter, the U.S. presence escalated. By the time the Nixon Administration withdrew U.S. forces in 1973, millions of U.S. troops had served in Vietnam, with more than 50,000 killed.

The war became increasingly unpopular in the United States and in Congress. In 1973, following the conclusion of a Paris Peace Agreement that brought an end to U.S. military involvement in Vietnam, Congress began cutting Nixon Administration requests for military and economic assistance to South Vietnam.

U.S.-Vietnam diplomatic and economic relations were virtually nonexistent for more than 15 years following North Vietnam's victory in 1975 over South Vietnam. The United States maintained a trade embargo and suspended foreign assistance to unified Vietnam.[14] Obstacles to improved relations included U.S. demands that Vietnam withdraw from Cambodia (which Vietnam invaded in 1978), U.S. insistence on the return of and information about U.S. Prisoners of War/Missing in Action (POW/MIAs), and Vietnamese demands that the United States provide several billion dollars in postwar reconstruction aid, which they claimed had been promised by the Nixon Administration.[15]

A series of actions by Vietnam following the end of the Vietnam War had a long-term negative effect on U.S.-Vietnamese relations. Stymied in its efforts to establish relations with the United States, Vietnam aligned itself economically and militarily with the Soviet Union. In addition, it invaded Cambodia and installed a government backed by 200,000 Vietnamese troops.[16] China conducted a one-month military incursion along Vietnam's northern border in 1979, which led to nearly three decades of disputes over the land border, and kept strong military pressure on Vietnam until 1990. U.S. policy toward Vietnam was also influenced by the exodus of hundreds of thousands of Vietnamese "boat people," including many ethnic Chinese, who fled or were expelled under Vietnam's harsh reunification program.

Developments in the mid- and late 1980s set the stage for the rapid normalization of ties in the following decade. Inside Vietnam, disastrous economic conditions and virtual diplomatic isolation led the VCP to adopt (at its 6th National Party Congress in 1986) a more pragmatic, less ideological, line. Hanoi adopted market-oriented economic reforms (dubbed *doi moi*, or "renovation"), loosened many domestic political controls, and began to seek ways to extract itself from Cambodia.

U.S.-Vietnam cooperation on the POW/MIA issue began to improve following a 1987 visit to Vietnam by General John Vessey, President Reagan's Special Emissary for POW-MIA Issues. As Vietnam withdrew forces from Cambodia in 1989 and sought a compromise peace settlement there, the George H. W. Bush Administration decided to improve relations with Hanoi, which was also interested in restoring ties to the United States. In April 1991, the United States laid out a detailed "road map" for normalization with Vietnam. Later that year, Vietnam allowed the United States to open an office in Hanoi to handle POW/MIA affairs.

---

[14] Congressional resistance to aiding Vietnam was strong for much of the 1970s. In the FY1977 foreign aid appropriations bill, Congress prohibited the use of any funds to provide assistance to Vietnam, a provision that was repeated annually until its removal in 1994. Earlier in the decade, President Richard Nixon's pledge to provide reconstruction aid to North Vietnam proved unpopular in Congress. *New York Times*, June 12, 1973.

[15] Vietnamese officials claimed that President Richard Nixon secretly had promised North Vietnamese Prime Minister Pham Van Dong $4.7 billion in economic assistance as part of the Paris Peace Agreement, signed in January 1973, which led to the withdrawal of U.S. troops from South Vietnam. *New York Times*, February 2, 1973; Nayan Chanda, *Brother Enemy* (New York: Harcourt Brace Jovanovich, 1986), p. 143.

[16] Among the reasons Vietnam invaded were Cambodia's incursions into Vietnamese territory after the Khmer Rouge took power in 1975. Additionally, among the atrocities the Khmer Rouge committed before they were ousted by the Vietnamese in 1949 were targeting ethnic Vietnamese as enemies of the state.

In 1993, President Clinton built on the thaw by signaling the end of U.S. opposition to Vietnam receiving international financial assistance. In February 1994, President Clinton announced the end of the U.S. trade embargo on Vietnam. Two months later, Congress passed the Foreign Relations Authorization Act, Fiscal Years 1994 and 1995 (P.L. 103-236), which contained a "Sense of the Senate" section expressing that chamber's support for the normalization of relations with Vietnam. Despite congressional efforts to tie normalization to the POW/MIA issue and Vietnam's human rights record, President Clinton continued to advance U.S. relations with Vietnam. He appointed the first post-war ambassador to Vietnam in 1997 and signed the landmark U.S.-Vietnam bilateral trade agreement (BTA) in 2000. Throughout this period, the normalization process was made possible by Vietnam's strategic desire to improve relations with the United States, continued improvements in POW/MIA cooperation, Vietnam's ongoing reform efforts, and by Vietnam's general cooperation on refugee issues. President Clinton visited Vietnam from November 16-20, 2000, the first trip by a U.S. President since Richard Nixon went to Saigon (now Ho Chi Minh City) in 1969. The visit was notable for the unexpected enthusiasm expressed by ordinary Vietnamese, who thronged by the thousands to greet or catch a glimpse of the President and the First Lady. These spontaneous outbursts, combined with the President's public and private remarks about human rights and democratization, triggered rhetorical responses from conservative Vietnamese leaders. During the visit, Vietnamese leaders pressed the United States for compensation for Agent Orange victims, for assistance locating the remains of Vietnam's soldiers still missing, and for an increase in the United States' bilateral economic assistance program.

Progress towards the resumption of normal bilateral relations continued under the George W. Bush Administration. Despite growing concerns about the Vietnamese government's human rights record, Congress ratified the U.S.-Vietnam BTA in October 2001 and the new agreement went into effect on December 10, 2001. Under the BTA, the United States granted Vietnam *conditional* normal trade relations (NTR), a move that significantly reduced U.S. tariffs on most imports from Vietnam.[17] In return, Hanoi agreed to undertake a wide range of market-liberalization measures. Vietnam's conditional NTR status was renewed every year until December 2006, when Congress passed P.L. 109-432, a comprehensive trade and tax bill, which granted Vietnam permanent NTR status as part of a wider agreement that saw Vietnam become a member of the World Trade Organization (WTO) as of January 11, 2007.[18]

During the Bush Administration, the United States and Vietnam dramatically upgraded diplomatic and strategic aspects of their relationship to the point where the two countries had all-but-normalized bilateral relations, at least from the U.S. point of view. However, many Vietnamese still consider relations to not be completely normalized until the United States provides more compensation for purported victims of "Agent Orange" and/or drops its legal categorization of Vietnam as a non-market economy.

---

[17] Vietnam's NTR status was conditional because it was subject to annual presidential and congressional review under the U.S. Trade Act of 1974's Jackson-Vanik provisions, which govern trade with non-market economies. Every year between 1998 and 2006, Vietnam received a presidential waiver from the restrictions of the Jackson-Vanik provisions. From 1998 to 2002, congressional resolutions disapproving the waivers failed in the House. Disapproval resolutions were not introduced between 2003 and 2006, the last year of Vietnam's conditional NTR status.

[18] See CRS Report RL33490, *Vietnam PNTR Status and WTO Accession: Issues and Implications for the United States*, by Mark E. Manyin, William H. Cooper, and Bernard A. Gelb.

Major Issues in U.S.-Vietnam Relations

Diplomatic Ties

High Level Meetings, the July 2013 Summit, and the Comprehensive Partnership

In the middle of the last decade, leaders in both Hanoi and Washington, DC, sought new ways to upgrade the bilateral relationship. As part of this process, both countries began increasing the number, frequency, and breadth of high-level bilateral visits. During each of the four years of George W. Bush's second term, the United States and Vietnam held an annual summit. The Bush Administration appeared to use these top-level meetings to encourage economic and political reforms inside Vietnam, as well as to signal the two countries' budding partnership on strategic issues. During the Obama Administration, the intensity and frequency of high-level bilateral meetings have expanded.

Until 2013, an exception to frequent bilateral meetings was at the leaders' level (i.e. between the U.S. President and either the Vietnamese President or Prime Minister). For the first five years of his presidency, despite multiple trips to Southeast Asia and the desire of Vietnamese officials to hold a summit meeting, President Obama neither visited Vietnam nor held a standalone meeting with Vietnamese President Truong Tan Sang or Prime Minister Nguyen Tan Dung. The Obama Administration appeared to be reluctant to schedule one in part due to concerns about the perceived deterioration in Vietnam's human rights conditions.

This changed in July 2013, when President Barack Obama hosted a meeting at the White House with Vietnam's President Sang. It was President Sang's first trip to the United States. The two presidents announced a bilateral "comprehensive partnership" that is to provide an "overarching framework" for moving the relationship to a "new phase." Among other items, the partnership is to include an increase in high level exchanges, the conclusion of a TPP agreement, and the discussion of constructing new and improved embassies. The two sides agreed to create new mechanisms for cooperation across nine sectors.[19] Bilateral cooperation already has been underway, in some cases for years, in most of the items listed in each sector.[20] At the leaders' joint remarks following their meeting, President Sang announced that President Obama had agreed to "try his best" to visit Vietnam before the end of his term in office.

Both sides had sought the completion of an official partnership for years, but progress had stalled, apparently due to U.S. concerns about Vietnam's human rights situation and to some Vietnamese concerns about creating a perception in Vietnam and China that Hanoi was drawing too close to Washington. According to the two presidents, in their meeting they discussed progress in the TPP negotiations, maritime disputes in the South China Sea, Vietnam's human rights situation, people-

---

[19] The nine areas of cooperation are political and diplomatic relations; trade and economic ties; science and technology; education and training; environment and health; war legacy issues; defense and security; protection and promotion of human rights; and culture, sports, and tourism.

[20] The White House, "Joint Statement by President Barack Obama of the United States of America and President Truong Tan Sang of the Socialist Republic of Vietnam," July 25, 2013.

to-people ties, and war legacy issues.[21] The United States reportedly resisted Vietnam's push for declaring a "strategic partnership," which according to one analysis generally includes a multi-year plan of action and a high-level joint mechanism to oversee implementation across all sectors of cooperation.[22]

The South China Sea Dispute

Since 2007, even as Vietnam and China have deepened their ties, bilateral tensions have intensified over competing territorial claims in the South China Sea. China has taken a number of actions to assert its claims since 2007, including reportedly warning Western energy companies not to work with Vietnam to explore or drill in disputed waters, announcing plans to develop disputed islands as tourist destinations, cutting sonar cables trailed by seismic exploration vessels working in disputed waters for PetroVietnam, and in May 2014, positioning the large CNOOC oil and gas exploration rig in disputed waters. For its part, Vietnam also has stepped up its presence in the disputed areas. For instance, since 2005 Vietnam has been active in soliciting bids for the exploration and development of offshore oil and gas blocks off its central coast, in areas disputed with China, and Vietnam's last two Five Year Plans placed a strong emphasis on offshore energy development. Both Vietnam and China have seized fishing boats and harassed ships operating in the disputed waters.

Vietnam has been active in soliciting international support to pressure China not to act unilaterally on its claims. A primary target of the Vietnamese campaign has been the United States, which takes no position on the question of sovereignty over disputed South China Sea landmasses. Vietnamese officials tend to say that while they do not expect the United States to take sides in the dispute, it would be helpful if the United States did more to emphasize, through language or actions, that all parties to the dispute—including China—should adhere to common principles, such as promoting transparency, adhering to the rule of law, refraining from undertaking unilateral actions, and committing to the freedom of the seas and navigation.

In 2010, the Obama Administration dramatically raised its involvement in the South China Sea disputes. In July of that year, then-Secretary of State Clinton stated at that year's annual ASEAN Regional Forum gathering of foreign ministers from the Asia-Pacific region that freedom of navigation on the sea is a U.S. "national interest" and that the United States opposes the use or threat of force by any claimant. Clinton also said that "legitimate claims to maritime space in the South China Sea should be derived solely from legitimate claims to land features," which many interpreted as an attack on the basis for China's claims to the entire sea.[23] Since 2010, such remarks have become a staple of U.S. officials' statements on the South China Sea disputes, and U.S. policy since then has been to work with Asian countries like Vietnam to include the disputes on the agenda of regional fora. China generally objects to discussing maritime security issues in multilateral settings, preferring to deal with the matter bilaterally. Relatedly, the Obama Administration also has continued its policy of upgrading its defense ties with and the capacities of many Southeast Asian militaries, including with Vietnamese security forces.

---

[21] The White House, "Remarks by President Obama and President Truong Tan Sang of Vietnam after Bilateral Meeting," July 25, 2013.

[22] Carlyle A. Thayer, "The U.S.-Vietnam Comprehensive Partnership: What's in a Name?" Thayer Consultancy Background Brief, July 26, 2013.

[23] U.S. Department of State, "Secretary of State Hillary Rodham Clinton Remarks at Press Availability," National Convention Center, Hanoi, Vietnam, July 23, 2010.

U.S. Interests in the South China Sea[24]

The South China Sea is the site of some of the world's most complicated maritime territorial disputes. Roughly one and a half times the size of the Mediterranean Sea, it is ringed by Brunei, China, Indonesia, Malaysia, the Philippines, Taiwan, and Vietnam and dotted with hundreds of small islands, shoals, and reefs, some of them occupied by individual claimants. This creates myriad overlapping claims, based on differing interpretations of historical boundaries to landmasses in the region and differing interpretations of the United Nations Convention on the Law of the Sea (UNCLOS). For instance, the U.S. position is that neither UNCLOS nor historical state practice negates the right of military forces of all nations to conduct military activities in each other's 200-mile Exclusive Economic Zone (EEZ) without notification or consent. In contrast, China insists that reconnaissance activities undertaken without prior notification and without permission of the coastal state violate Chinese domestic law and international law, and Chinese authorities often have protested against U.S. maritime surveillance along China's coast.[25]

The United States is not a claimant in the South China Sea, and has consistently taken no position on specific territorial disputes in these waters. Instead, it has repeatedly asserted its own broad interests in freedom of navigation and regional stability, and supported multilateral dialogues that foster stability, particularly discussions since the early 1990s between China and Southeast Asian claimants over a Code of Conduct for disputants in the region.

East Asia's large economies rely on freedom of navigation in the South China Sea. Roughly two-thirds of South Korea's energy supplies, 60% of Japan's, and 60% of Taiwan's pass through it, as do 80% of China's oil imports.[26] U.S. strategic interests in the region include the maintenance of regional peace, freedom of operation and navigation including for U.S. surveillance vessels, the protection of substantial trading interests, and the promotion of economic development including offshore energy development and sustainable management of fishery stocks and other resources. The United States also seeks to encourage China's development as a responsible international actor while balancing and protecting the interests of U.S. allies and strategic partners in Southeast Asia.

The Lower Mekong Initiative

One aspect of the Obama Administration's upgrading its relationship with Vietnam involves forming partnerships in multilateral fora. One such group, created in 2009, is the Lower Mekong Initiative (LMI), comprised of the United States and the lower Mekong countries (i.e., Burma/Myanmar, Cambodia, Laos, Thailand, and Vietnam). The State Department describes the initiative as "the primary U.S.-led platform for advancing Mekong sub-regional integration" and boosting development among Cambodia, Laos, Thailand, and Vietnam (Burma joined the LMI in 2012).[27] To this end, the group aims to foster cooperation and capacity building among the members in the areas of agriculture and food security, "connectivity" (promoting physical, institutional, and people-to-people connections), education, energy security, the environment and water, and health.[28] Another motivation for the LMI is to monitor and coordinate responses to the construction of dams—particularly but not exclusively those being built in China—and other projects on the upper portions of the Mekong that are affecting the downriver countries. Foreign ministers from participating countries have held five meetings, the last during Secretary Kerry's July 2013 visit to Brunei to participate in the ASEAN Regional Forum meeting.

Initially, the LMI largely encompassed or overlapped with existing U.S. regional aid programs and did not represent a significant increase to existing levels of U.S. funding.[29] In July 2012, at

---

[24] Written by Ben Dolven, CRS Specialist in Asian Affairs.

[25] For more, see Bonnie S. Glaser, *Armed Clash in the South China Sea*, Council on Foreign Relations Center for Preventive Action Contingency Planning Memorandum No. 14, April 2012.

[26] Ibid.

[27] "Rebalance to the Asia-Pacific," November 2012 State Department communication with CRS.

[28] Department of State, Lower Mekong Initiative, http://www.state.gov/p/eap/mekong/.

[29] Department of State, "Fact Sheet: Lower Mekong Initiative Progress 2010/11," July 22, 2011.

the ASEAN Regional Forum in Phnom Penh, then-Secretary of State Clinton announced the creation of the Asia Pacific Strategic Engagement Initiative (APSEI), which would significantly expand LMI programming. The first stage of the Initiative included a three-year, $50 million program, the "Lower Mekong Initiative 2020."[30] LMI 2020 is coordinated by the USAID regional office in Bangkok, Thailand, and administered largely through East Asia and Pacific (EAP) regional programs and the Regional Development Mission-Asia (RDM/A). The Obama Administration expects to spend around $16.2 million for LMI programs in FY2014 and has requested $10.4 million for FY2015.[31]

Economic Ties[32]

Economic ties arguably are the most mature aspect of the bilateral relationship, as symbolized by the two countries' participation in the TPP negotiations. Since the mid-2000s, the United States has been Vietnam's largest single-country export market; in 2013, exports to the United States represented about 18% of Vietnam's total exports.[33] However, China is Vietnam's single largest trading partner. By value, nearly 30% of Vietnam's imports in 2013 came from China.[34] Collectively, U.S. firms have become one of the country's largest sources of foreign direct investment (FDI). Since 2002, Vietnam has run an overall current account deficit with the rest of the world, though strong export growth in 2012 and 2013 narrowed the gap to near zero in 2013.

U.S.-Vietnam trade has soared since the early 2000s. As shown in **Table 1**, trade flows were nearly $30 billion in 2013, more than three times the level they were in 2006, the year before the United States restored permanent normal trade relations status to Vietnam. Increased bilateral trade also has been fostered by Vietnam's market-oriented reforms and the resulting growth in its foreign-invested and privately owned sectors. Over the last three years, Congress has appropriated approximately $10 million each year to support Vietnam's economic reforms. Most of the increase in U.S.-Vietnam trade since 2001 has come from the growth in imports from Vietnam, particularly clothing items. Indeed, Vietnam has emerged as the United States' second-largest source of imported clothing, after China, and is a major source for footwear, furniture, and electrical machinery.

---

[30] "Clinton Talks Cash Injections at ASEAN," *Phnom Penh Post*, July 12, 2012; Department of State, "Fact Sheet: Asia-Pacific Strategic Engagement Initiative, July 13, 2012.

[31] Statement of Joseph Y. Yun, Acting Assistant Secretary for East Asian and Pacific Affairs, before the House Foreign Affairs Committee, Subcommittee on Asia and the Pacific, May 16, 2013.

[32] For more, see CRS Report R41550, *U.S.-Vietnam Economic and Trade Relations: Issues for the 113th Congress*, by Michael F. Martin.

[33] General Statistics Office of Vietnam Press Release, "Socio-Economic Situation in 2013," December 27, 2013. Vietnam's exports to the 28-member European Union in 2013 were slightly more than its exports to the United States.

[34] Ibid.

Table 1. U.S.-Vietnam Merchandise Trade, Selected Years

millions of U.S. dollars

	U.S. Imports from Vietnam	U.S. Exports to Vietnam	Total Trade		Trade Balance
			Volume	Change from Prior Year	
2000	827.4	330.5	1,157.9	—	-496.9
2002 (NTR extended)a	2,391.7	551.9	2,943.6	107%	-1,839.8
2005	6,522.3	1,151.3	7,673.6	22%	-5,371.0
2006	8,463.4	988.4	9,451.8	23%	-7,475.0
2007 (PNTR Extended)a	10,541.2	1,823.3	12,364.5	31%	-8,717.9
2010	14,867.7	3,710.2	18,577.9	21.2%	-11,157.5
2012	20,265.9	4,623.3	24,889.2	14.0%	-15,642.6
2013	24,649.0	5,013.0	29,662.0	19.2%	-19,636.0

Source: U.S. International Trade Commission. Data are for merchandise trade on a customs basis.

a. Normal trade relations (NTR) status was extended to Vietnam in December 2001, when the U.S.-Vietnam bilateral trade agreement went into effect. Thus, 2002 was the first full year in which Vietnam benefitted from NTR status. Likewise, 2007 was the first full year Vietnam received permanent normal trade relations (PNTR) status, which was extended to Vietnam in December 2006.

Trade Initiatives: GSP, TIFA, BIT, and TPP

Vietnam has applied for acceptance into the U.S. Generalized System of Preferences (GSP) program and is participating in negotiations toward a Bilateral Investment Treaty (BIT) with the United States.[35] The United States also has expressed an interest in closer economic relations, but has told Vietnam that it needs to make certain changes in the legal, regulatory, and operating environment of its economy to conclude the BIT agreement, as well as to qualify for the GSP program. Legislation submitted in the 113th Congress, H.R. 1682 (Lofgren), would prohibit Vietnam's entry into the GSP program unless the Vietnamese government made certain improvements in the human rights and trafficking in persons arenas.

The most ambitious trade initiative with Vietnam involves negotiating a multilateral free trade agreement under the TPP.[36] According to many sources, Vietnam's presence in the talks has created challenges because in contrast to most other participants it is a developing economy with considerable government intervention. As part of its desire to use the TPP talks to achieve greater access to the U.S. market, Vietnam is trying to persuade the United States to accept more liberal rules of origin for clothing and textile trade, among other items. U.S. and other backers of Vietnam's participation in the negotiations believe that it further opens a sizeable market to U.S.

---

[35] The primary purpose of the GSP program, which the United States and other industrial countries initiated in the 1970s, is to promote economic growth and development in developing countries by stimulating their exports. For more, see CRS Report RL34702, *Potential Trade Effects of Adding Vietnam to the Generalized System of Preferences Program*, by Vivian C. Jones and Michael F. Martin.

[36] For more, see CRS Report R42694, *The Trans-Pacific Partnership (TPP) Negotiations and Issues for Congress*, coordinated by Ian F. Fergusson.

exports and investments, could accelerate economic reforms in Vietnam, and could set a precedent for the entry into the agreement of other countries, such as China, with sizeable government intervention in their economies.

Trade Friction

As bilateral economic relations have expanded, so have trade disputes. Significant areas of friction include clothing trade, fish (particularly catfish), the United States' designation of Vietnam as a "non-market economy" (NME), and Vietnam's record on protecting intellectual rights.[37] Trade in catfish has been particularly controversial, both with Vietnam and within the United States. In 2008, in response to continued growth in imports of catfish-like fish (called tra and basa) from Vietnam, the 110th Congress passed legislation that transferred the regulation of catfish from the Food and Drug Administration (FDA) to the U.S. Department of Agriculture (USDA), which generally is viewed as maintaining stricter inspection standards than the FDA. The Agricultural Act of 2014 (P.L. 113-79) included language that confirmed the inspection transfer to USDA, as well as defined catfish to include basa and tra exported from Vietnam. The Vietnamese government strongly protested these actions as largely protectionist measures. In general, while bilateral trade disputes have been irritants, as of mid-2014 they have not spilled over to affect the course or tone of bilateral relations.

U.S. Foreign Assistance to Vietnam

As the normalization process has proceeded, the United States has eliminated most of the Cold War-era restrictions on aid to Vietnam. U.S. assistance has increased markedly from the approximately $1 million that was provided when assistance was resumed in 1991. Annual aid levels increased steadily during the 1990s, rising to the $20 million level by 2000. The George W. Bush Administration raised bilateral assistance by an order or magnitude—aid surpassed $100 million by the late 2000s—and made Vietnam one of the largest recipients of U.S. aid in East Asia. U.S. assistance to Vietnam in FY2011 was over $140 million. For FY2014, the Obama Administration expects to spend over $100 million on aid programs in Vietnam. Most of the decline comes from reduced spending on programs to combat HIV/AIDS and to promote market-oriented reforms. In recent years, some Members of Congress have attempted to link increases in non-humanitarian aid to progress in Vietnam's human rights record (see the "Human Rights Issues" section).

The U.S. bilateral aid program has been dominated by health-related assistance. In particular, spending on HIV/AIDS treatment and prevention in Vietnam has risen since President Bush designated Vietnam as a "focus country" eligible to receive increased funding to combat HIV/AIDS in June 2004 under the President's Emergency Plan for AIDS Relief (PEPFAR).[38] Some Vietnamese, as well as some Western aid providers, have questioned the wisdom of allocating these sums of money for Vietnam, which does not appear to have a severe HIV/AIDS

---

[37] Under the terms of its entry into the WTO, Vietnam will retain its designation as a "non-market economy" (NME) until 2019, making it procedurally easier in many cases for U.S. companies to initiate and succeed in bringing anti-dumping cases against Vietnamese exports. Vietnamese officials would like the United States to recognize Vietnam as a market economy.

[38] Vietnam qualified for the designation in part because of its demonstrated commitment to fighting the epidemic on its own and because of the competency of its medical institutions. Vietnam is estimated to have about 100,000 people living with the HIV/AIDS virus, a number that is projected to grow significantly.

problem. Other sizeable U.S. assistance items include programs assisting Vietnam's economic reform efforts and governance, programs to combat trafficking in persons, and de-mining programs. Cumulatively, since 2007 Congress has appropriated over $100 million for dioxin removal and related health care services (for more details, see the "Agent Orange" section).

The governments of the United States and Vietnam run a number of educational exchange programs. These generally total around $10 million a year, a sum not included in the above estimates of U.S. assistance.

Human Rights Issues

Overview

Vietnam is a one-party, authoritarian state. The government security organs maintain an extensive surveillance network throughout the country that allows it to monitor the daily activities of Vietnamese citizens when it chooses to do so. For more than a decade, the Vietnamese Communist Party (VCP) appears to have followed a strategy of informally permitting (while not necessarily legalizing) most forms of personal and religious expression while selectively repressing individuals and organizations that it deems a threat to the party's monopoly on power. On the one hand, the gradual loosening of restrictions since Vietnam's *doi moi* ("renovation") economic reforms were launched in 1986 has opened the door for Vietnamese to engage in private enterprise and has permitted most Vietnamese to observe the religion of their choice.

On the other hand, the authorities crack down harshly on what they deem to be anti-government activity. According to numerous accounts, since at least early 2007 the Vietnamese government's suppression of dissent has intensified and its tolerance for criticism has lessened markedly. These trends appear to have continued into the first half of 2014, particularly with ongoing arrests of Internet activists, notwithstanding the government's release of some high-profile political prisoners in the early spring.[39] As opposed to a massive suppression, the Vietnamese government's actions appear to be selective, targeting specific individuals and organizations that have called for the institution of democratic reforms and/or publicly criticized government policy on sensitive issues, such as policy toward China. The government increasingly has targeted bloggers and lawyers who represent human rights and religious freedom activists, particularly those linked to pro-democracy activist networks. Many of the targeted blogs, bloggers, and lawyers have criticized Vietnam's policy toward China and/or have links to pro-democracy activist groups.

More dissident groups began to appear publicly beginning in 2006. It is unclear to what extent these groups or their various goals are supported by the broader Vietnamese public. Most analysts believe that the pro-democracy movement in Vietnam is much too weak to pose any systemic threat to the VCP. However, the government's heightened sensitivity and stiffened response may be due to its concerns about growing public discontent over alleged government corruption, land

---

[39] In his June 2014 confirmation hearing to become Ambassador to Vietnam, Ambassador-designate Ted Osius said that since the announcement of the July 2013 comprehensive partnership, Vietnam had made "some progress" in human rights issues. Osius cited Vietnam's signing of a United Nations convention against torture, publishing of an International Labour Organization report on forced labor and child labor, and releasing of "a small number of prisoners." CQ Congressional Transcripts, "Senate Foreign Relations Committee Holds Confirmation Hearing on Various Ambassadorial and U.S. Agency for International Development Nominations," June 17, 2014.

seizures by government institutions and officials, worsened economic conditions, and a sense among some Vietnamese that Hanoi has been unable to prevent China from asserting its maritime claims at Vietnam's expense. Additionally, reported power struggles among Vietnam's top leaders may be contributing to the intensified crackdown.

Human Rights in U.S.-Vietnam Relations

In general, differences over human rights between the U.S. and Vietnamese governments have not prevented the two countries from improving the overall relationship. Barring a dramatic downturn in Vietnam's human rights situation, Obama Administration officials appear to see Vietnam's human rights situation not as an impediment to short-term cooperation on various issues, but rather as establishing a ceiling on what might be accomplished. In the view of some policymakers and observers, the two countries increasingly are bumping up against this ceiling.

Over the past four years, criticisms of Vietnam's human rights record, including from some Members of Congress, appear to have played a significant role in convincing the Administration to oppose a number of items desired by Hanoi, including expanding the types of arms that U.S. companies can sell to Vietnam. Additionally, concerns about Vietnam's human rights record are likely to complicate Congress' debate over a TPP agreement, if the current negotiations are successful. It is unclear to what extent—if at all—the Obama Administration has attempted to use the TPP negotiations as a way to encourage Vietnamese officials to make changes in its human rights regime. If applied, such pressure is unlikely in the view of some to have much impact unless and until a final TPP agreement begins to take shape.

Press and Internet Freedoms

Vietnam has a variety of newspapers and magazines available, but virtually all of them are published by government or party organizations. For example, *Thanh Nien*, a leading daily newspaper, is published by the Vietnam National Youth Federation. In recent years, Vietnam's press has demonstrated a greater willingness to cover stories and issues that could be controversial or risk post-publication reprisals from the Vietnamese government, such as allegations of official corruption or incompetence. At times, the Vietnamese government appears to appreciate these stories, if they support the Party's specific efforts to target particular instances of corruption among VCP and government officials. However, a journalist or publication that crosses the vague and fluid boundary of acceptability to Party leaders frequently faces official retribution, including loss of job, temporary closure, fines, and possibly imprisonment.

Besides increasingly targeting journalists and bloggers, the Vietnamese government also has brought charges against lawyers who have represented the accused in court or have spoken out against the Vietnamese government. Many of the targeted blogs, bloggers, and lawyers criticized Vietnam's policy toward China and/or have links to pro-democracy activist groups such as Bloc 8406, the banned Democratic Party of Vietnam, or the banned Independent Workers' Union of Vietnam. There are reports that these groups have received help from expatriate Vietnamese, including some in the United States, a charge that Vietnamese officials often make in conversations with their U.S. counterparts.

Ethnic Minorities

Ethnic minorities account for the majority of the population in three regions of the country: the Central Highlands (home to Montagnard groups), the Northwest Highlands (Hmong), and along portions of the Mekong Delta in the south (Khmer). A number of these minority groups report cases of discrimination, which the State Department calls "longstanding and persistent," and repression.[40] The situations in all three regions are complicated. In each, the individuals and groups that frequently clash with government authorities are often ethnic minorities, belong to religious groups (such as Protestant denominations) that are not legally recognized by the government, and/or at various points in history have opposed being ruled by Vietnam's dominant ethnic group (the Kinh) and/or by the communist government.

Many of the larger-scale tensions between the government and minority groups occur because of protests against land seizures by local government officials. Indeed, corruption related to inappropriate land taking and use is one of the most sensitive and problematic issues for Vietnam. In Vietnam, the state owns the land on behalf of the people of Vietnam. Residents and investors can buy and sell "land-use rights," but the government legally can reclaim land, often with allegedly low levels of compensation. Many of the larger-scale tensions between the government and minority groups (including religious minorities) occur when land used by these groups— which already feel they have been the victims of discrimination, harassment, or worse—is seized by local government officials, some of whom allegedly personally profit from the transaction. According to several sources, abuses against the "Montagnards" who live in the country's Central Highlands region appear to have fallen since the last major anti-government protests in 2004. Various government programs have attempted to improve educational and economic opportunities for minorities in the region.[41] (For the location of the Central Highlands region, see **Figure 1** at the end of this report.) However, accurate reporting is complicated by restrictions on foreigners' access to the region and ability to meet freely with Montagnards who have fled to Cambodia. No major demonstrations appear to have taken place in the Central Highlands since 2008. Some human rights advocates have criticized the U.S. government for failing to advocate sufficiently for the release of the scores, if not hundreds, of Montagnards whom Vietnamese authorities have imprisoned since 2001, as well as for the dozens of Montagnards who have fled to Thailand seeking asylum in a third country. Additionally, some Montagnard Americans have complained that the Vietnamese authorities either have prevented them from visiting Vietnam or have been subjected to interrogation upon re-entering the country on visits. As for the Northwest Highlands, in 2011, Vietnamese authorities reportedly forcibly suppressed protests by ethnic Hmong, the first such unrest in that region in years.

Reports of abuses against ethnic Khmer in the Mekong Delta region peaked in 2007 and 2008, when widespread protests erupted against local government land seizures. There do not appear to have been large-scale demonstrations or protests since that time, though it is unclear whether this

---

[40] State Department, *Country Reports on Human Rights Practices for 2013, Vietnam.*

[41] "Montagnard" is a French term meaning "mountain people" that is often used to refer to the various indigenous ethnic minorities in Vietnam's central and northern mountain areas. According to Human Rights Watch, there are approximately one million Montagnards in the Central Highlands, comprised of approximately six ethnic groups. Since the end of the Vietnam War, millions of ethnic Kinh (Vietnam's dominant ethnic group) from Vietnam's lowlands have migrated into the Central Highlands. Coffee and rubber plantations also have sprouted in the region. The ensuing land pressures have resulted the loss of ancestral homeland by many Montagnards. Hundreds of thousands of Central Highlands Montagnards are thought to be evangelical Protestants.

is due to the resolution of the underlying issues or to the government's crackdown against the protest leaders.

Religious Freedom

Buddhism is the dominant religion in Vietnam, comprising approximately half of the population, according to the State Department. An estimated 7% of the population is Roman Catholic, which is concentrated in the southern part of the country. Other religious groupings include Cao Dai organizations (2.5%-4.0%), Hoa Hao (the one officially recognized sect comprises 1.5%-3.0% of the population), and Protestant groups (recognized groups comprise 1%-2%).[42]

According to a variety of reports, most Vietnamese now are able to observe the religion of their choice in accordance with Vietnamese laws and regulations governing religious observance, which require religious groups to be officially recognized and registered. However, while the freedom to worship generally exists in Vietnam, the government strictly regulates and monitors the activities of religious organizations. Periodically, authorities have increased restrictions on certain groups. Although the constitution provides for freedom of religion, Vietnamese law requires religious groups to be officially recognized or registered. According to many reports, the government uses this process to monitor and restrict religious organizations' operations. Additionally, many groups either refuse to join one of the official religious orders or are denied permission to do so, meaning that these groups' activities technically are illegal. This legal status can make their leaders and practitioners vulnerable to arrest and harassment. Human Rights Watch and other groups have reported harassment over the past three years against a number of unrecognized branches of several faiths, including the Cao Dai church; the Hoa Hao Buddhist church; independent Protestant house churches (particularly in the Central Highlands); Khmer Krom Buddhist temples in the Mekong Delta; and the Unified Buddhist Church of Vietnam (UBCV).[43]

Disputes between the government and religious groups have been growing in recent years over the seizure of church and temple land by local governments. Many of these cases involve recent confiscations for both civic reasons (e.g., public works projects) and also for resale that allegedly benefits local government officials and/or their families.

Some noted religious figures in Vietnam are politically active. When such figures are subjected to official abuse, it is not always clear whether they are targeted for their religious or political activism. For example, Roman Catholic priest Father Nguyen Van Ly is one of a number of prominent religious leaders who have also been vocal in their opposition to the VCP and their support for multi-party democracy, and as a result, have been convicted of crimes against the Vietnamese government.[44]

In 2004, the State Department designated Vietnam as a "country of particular concern" (CPC), principally because of reports of worsening harassment of certain ethnic minority Protestants and Buddhists. When the Vietnamese responded by negotiating with the Bush Administration and

---

[42] State Department, *International Religious Freedom Report for 2012: Vietnam*."

[43] Human Rights Watch, "EU–Vietnam Human Rights Dialogue: Human Rights Watch Recommendations," January 10, 2012.

[44] Among other charges, in 2007, Father Ly was re-arrested and subsequently sentenced to eight years' imprisonment for violating laws against "conducting propaganda against the state" due to his role in cofounding Bloc 8406.

adopting internal changes, the two sides reached an agreement on religious freedom, in which Hanoi agreed to take steps to improve conditions for people of faith, particularly in the Central Highlands. The May 2005 agreement enabled Vietnam to avoid punitive consequences, such as sanctions, associated with its CPC designation. The agreement was faulted by human rights groups on a number of grounds, including the charge that religious persecution continues in the Central Highlands. Vietnam was redesignated a CPC in the 2005 and 2006 Religious Freedom Reports.

In November 2006, the State Department announced that because of "many positive steps" taken by the Vietnamese government since 2004, the country was no longer a "severe violator of religious freedom" and was removed from the CPC list. The announcement, which came two days before President Bush was due to depart to Hanoi for the APEC summit, cited a dramatic decline in forced renunciations of faith, the release of religious prisoners, an expansion of freedom to organize by many religious groups, and the issuance of new laws and regulations, and stepped up enforcement mechanisms. Over the course of 2006, as part of the bilateral U.S.-Vietnam human rights dialogue, Vietnam released a number of prominent dissidents the Bush Administration had identified as "prisoners of concern." Vietnam also reportedly told the United States that it would repeal its administrative decree allowing detention without trial. The U.S. Committee on International Religious Freedom, among others, disputed the Administration's factual basis for the decision to remove Vietnam from the CPC list, arguing that abuses continue and that lifting the CPC label removes an incentive for Vietnam to make further improvements. Members of Congress introduced several pieces of legislation that have called on the State Department to re-list Vietnam as a CPC.[45]

Workers' Rights[46]

Vietnam's participation in the TPP trade negotiations and application to join the GSP program have focused attention on labor conditions in Vietnam. The government and the VCP's efforts to maintain one-party rule while adapting to rapid social and economic changes may help to explain the often contradictory trends that can be observed in Vietnam's evolving labor rights regime.

The U.S. government and a number of non-governmental organizations (NGOs) such as Human Rights Watch have been critical of Vietnam's restrictions on workers' rights. There is a general recognition that Vietnam has made significant improvements in its labor laws, but that local government enforcement and business compliance remain ongoing problems. The State Department's 2013 human rights report on Vietnam singled out problems with suppression of independent labor unions, failure to enforce laws governing the right to organize, forced or compulsory labor, child labor, and unacceptable working conditions.

Workers in Vietnam have the legal right to collective bargaining. At present, all labor unions in Vietnam must be a member of the Vietnam General Confederation of Labor (VGCL). The VGCL is supposed to organize a union within six months of the establishment of any new business, regardless of its ownership—state, foreign, or private. Human Rights Watch also has raised

---

[45] During the 111th Congress the House passed one such measure, H.Res. 20.

[46] The bulk of this section was written by Michael Martin, CRS Specialist in Asian Affairs.

concern about the ability of Vietnamese workers to call an official strike, especially at state-owned enterprises (SOEs).[47]

Vietnamese workers are not legally allowed to form unions independent of the VGCL, and efforts to organize independent unions in Vietnam reportedly have been thwarted by government suppression, including the arrest and imprisonment of union leaders. Some analysts have argued that restrictions of the right of association in Vietnam have impeded the improvement of labor rights in other areas. According to some reports, there were signs that the aforementioned May 2014 riots against foreign-owned firms in industrial areas near Ho Chi Minh City were partly motivated by workers' frustrations with factory conditions.[48]

Other observers, however, counter that since the launch of *doi moi*, worker rights have made progress despite the restrictions on the independent right to organize. These observers point out that hundreds of unaffiliated (and therefore unofficial) "labor associations" have sprouted without significant repression, that the VGCL has evolved into a more aggressive advocate for workers, and in many recent cases, Vietnamese workers have gone on strike reportedly because they felt that they were not well-represented by the official union. The State Department reports that in the first half of 2013, the Vietnamese government took "no action" against the more than 150 strikes that occurred, despite the fact that none were technically legal.[49]

Human Trafficking[50]

Vietnam is both a source and destination for people trafficked for forced labor and commercial sexual exploitation. Additionally, state-owned and private labor export companies send tens of thousands of Vietnamese construction, fishing, and manufacturing workers overseas, where many are vulnerable to abuse and exploitation. Among Asian expatriate workers, Vietnamese reportedly incur some of the highest debts, due among other factors to high recruitment fees.[51]

Since 2001, the first year in which the State Department issued a Trafficking in Persons (TIP) Report pursuant to the Trafficking Victims Protect Act, as amended (TVPA, Div. A of P.L. 106-386), Vietnam has variously been designated a "Tier 2" (in 2001-2003, 2005-2009, and 2012) or a "Tier 2 Watch List" (in 2004, 2010, and 2011) country. In the 2012 TIP report, Vietnam's tier ranking improved to "Tier 2," a ranking the 2013 and 2014 reports maintained. Countries designated as Tier 2 do not fully comply with the minimum standards to eliminate severe forms of human trafficking, but are making significant efforts to do so. Vietnam's elevation to Tier 2 status in the 2012 TIP Report was due in large part to the adoption of a new law to prevent and combat human trafficking in March 2011 and the completion of a five-year national action plan to combat human trafficking. The new law went into effect on January 1, 2012, and included an expanded list of prohibited trafficking-related acts. The 2014 TIP report listed the government's prosecution and conviction of some transnational sex trafficking offenders, as well as the issuance of regulations under the 2012 trafficking law, as evidence that it is making "significant efforts" to

---

[47] Human Rights Watch, *Not Yet a Workers' Paradise*, New York, NY, May 2009.

[48] Joshua Kurlantzick, "Vietnam Protests: More Than Just Anti-China Sentiment," *Asia Unbound*, Council on Foreign Relations blog, May 15, 2014.

[49] State Department, Country Reports on Human Rights Practices for 2013, Vietnam.

[50] This section was written by Liana Wyler, CRS Analyst in International Crime and Narcotics.

[51] State Department, 2014 Trafficking in Persons Report, pp. 408-410.

comply with the minimum standards for eliminating trafficking. H.R. 1897/S. 1649, the Vietnam Human Rights Act, contains a sense of the Congress provision declaring that Vietnam's activities to combat human trafficking are insufficient to justify its "Tier 2" status.

The Vietnam Human Rights Act

Since the 107th Congress, when Members of Congress became concerned with Vietnamese government crackdowns against protestors in the Central Highlands region, various legislative attempts have been made to link U.S. assistance to the human rights situation in Vietnam. A number of measures entitled "The Vietnam Human Rights Act" have been introduced, with most proposing to cap existing non-humanitarian U.S. assistance programs to the Vietnamese government at existing levels if the President does not certify that Vietnam is making "substantial progress" in human rights.[52]

As introduced, the most recent version of the Vietnam Human Rights Act (H.R. 1897/S. 1649 in the 113th Congress) would prohibit increases in many forms of U.S. non-humanitarian assistance to the Vietnamese government unless (a) Vietnam's human rights conditions are certified as improving, or (b) the President issues a waiver.[53] The bill explicitly exempts specific categories of assistance such as dioxin remediation and HIV/AIDS programs, and it would grant the President waiver authority that allows him to exempt any programs that are deemed to promote the goals of the act and/or to be in the national interests of the United States. Among other items, H.R. 1897/S. 1649 also state that the sense of Congress is that the United States should not reduce Vietnamese language services of the Voice of America and Radio Free Asia; that Vietnam should be redesignated as a country of particular concern for religious freedom; and that Vietnam's activities to combat human trafficking are insufficient to justify its elevation to "Tier 2" status in the State Department's annual trafficking in persons report. The act would require the State Department to file an annual report to Congress on various items. The House passed H.R. 1897 on August 1, 2013, by a vote of 405-3 (Roll Call 435).

Proponents of the Vietnam Human Rights Act argue that additional pressure should be placed on the Vietnamese government to improve its human rights record. Critics have argued that the bill could chill the warming of bilateral political and security ties and could weaken economic reformers in ongoing domestic political battles inside Vietnam.

---

[52] The Vietnam Human Rights Act was first introduced in the 107th Congress as H.R. 2833, which was passed by the House, 410-1 (roll call 335) on September 6, 2001, and did not receive action in the Senate. In the 108th Congress, H.R. 1587 and S. 2784 were introduced. The House passed H.R. 1587 by a vote of 323-45 (roll call 391). In the Senate, the bill was not reported out of committee, and attempts to include an abbreviated version in an omnibus appropriation bill did not succeed. In the 109th Congress, another stripped-down version of the act (H.R. 3190) was included in the House-passed version of the Foreign Relations Authorization Act of FY2006/FY2007 (H.R. 2601), which did not receive action in the Senate. In the 110th Congress, the House passed H.R. 3096 on September 18, 2007 (414-3, roll no. 877). The bill did not see action in the Senate. Also in the 110th, a competing version of the Vietnam Human Rights Act, S. 3678, was introduced in the Senate. In the 111th Congress, H.R. 1969 and S. 1159 were introduced by did not see action. In the 112th Congress, the House passed by voice vote H.R. 1410, which did not see action in the Senate.

[53] Previous versions of the act had included a provision requiring increases in non-humanitarian assistance to the Vietnamese government unless such increases in aid were matched by increases in funding for certain types of human rights, rule of law, and anti-jamming programs.

Military-to-Military Ties

At the end of the previous decade, the United States and Vietnam began upgrading their military-to-military relationship, driven in large measure by Vietnam's increased concerns about China and enabled by over a decade of smaller, trust-building programs between the two military bureaucracies. In the 1990s, the bulk of military-to-military cooperation consisted of programs dealing with "legacy" issues from the Vietnam War era. Notably, the two militaries developed a cooperative relationship in locating the remains of U.S. missing servicemen. Since at least the early 2000s, the Pentagon and State Department began seeking to expand and deepen security relations and military ties with Vietnam. More than a decade later, many of these efforts have borne fruit. An International Military Education and Training (IMET) agreement was signed in 2005, followed two years later by the United States allowing sales of non-lethal defense items to Vietnam. In August 2010, the United States and Vietnam held their inaugural Defense Policy Dialogue, a high-level channel for direct military-to-military discussions. Previously, the main formal vehicle for the two militaries to hold regular annual dialogues had been through the U.S.-Vietnam Security Dialogue on Political, Security, and Defense Issues, a forum that is run by the U.S. State Department and Vietnamese Ministry of Foreign Affairs and includes officials from the two countries' militaries. Other signs of a deepening military-military relationship include U.S.-Vietnam joint naval engagements (involving noncombat training), Vietnamese shipyards repairing U.S. noncombatant naval vessels, cooperation in peacekeeping and search-and-rescue training operations, and the Vietnamese Ministry of Defense sending Vietnamese officers to U.S. staff colleges and other military institutions. Notwithstanding these developments, the evolution of bilateral military ties has come incrementally and more slowly than many U.S. military planners would prefer. Vietnamese military officials generally have been resistant to taking major steps forward, perhaps due to a concern of alarming China.

Military Assistance

The United States-Vietnam IMET agreement allows Vietnamese officers to receive English language training in the United States. In 2007, the United States modified International Traffic in Arms Regulations (ITAR) regarding Vietnam by allowing licenses for trade in certain non-lethal defense items and services to Vietnam. Such transactions are reviewed on a case-by-case basis. In FY2009, the United States provided foreign military financing (FMF) for Vietnam for the first time. According to annual State Department reports covering fiscal years 2007-2010, the department licensed the export of approximately $98.5 million of defense articles and $3.7 million of defense services to Vietnam during that time. Regarding foreign military sales (FMS), according to the State Department, Vietnam has submitted letters of request for helicopter spare parts and English language labs.[54] In FY2009, the United States extended foreign military financing (FMF) for the Vietnamese government for the first time. According to State Department officials, "very little" of the approved FMF has been spent, with most going toward English training labs/instructors, spare parts for helicopters, and ship radios.[55] As mentioned earlier, in December 2013 the United States said it would provide Vietnam with $18 million in assistance, including five fast patrol vessels, to enhance Vietnam's maritime security capacity.

---

[54] September 2011 e-mail correspondence with State Department officials.

[55] September 2011 e-mail correspondence with State Department officials.

Vietnamese leaders have asked the Obama Administration and Members of Congress to remove U.S. restrictions on lethal weapons sales to Vietnam, and have stated that they will not consider bilateral relations to be fully normalized until that decision is taken.[56] Under questioning from Senator John McCain during his June confirmation hearing to be Ambassador to Vietnam, Ted Osius said that because Vietnam had made "some progress" in improving selected human rights conditions, it "may mean it's time to begin exploring the possibility of lifting the ban" on lethal weapons sales. When asked for more explanation, Osius added, "what we haven't done is lay out a precise roadmap for what would get the Vietnamese to lifting the lethal weapons ban. And it may be time to consider that."[57]

Vietnam War "Legacy" Issues

Agent Orange[58]

One major legacy of the Vietnam War that remains unresolved is the damage that Agent Orange, and its accompanying dioxin, has done to the people and the environment of Vietnam. According to various estimates, the U.S. military sprayed approximately 11-12 million gallons of Agent Orange over nearly 10% of then-South Vietnam between 1961 and 1971. One scientific study estimated that between 2.1 million and 4.8 million Vietnamese were directly exposed to Agent Orange. Vietnamese advocacy groups claim that there are over three million Vietnamese suffering from serious health problems caused by exposure to the dioxin in Agent Orange.

In the past, this issue generally was pushed to the background of bilateral discussions by other issues considered more important by the United States and/or Vietnam. As the relationship has improved and matured, and with most other wartime "legacy" issues now resolved, the issue of Agent Orange/dioxin has emerged as a regular topic in bilateral discussions and is one to which several Members of Congress have brought attention. Recently, the U.S. government has shown a greater willingness to cooperate on some aspects of the issue. Since 2007, Congress has appropriated nearly $110 million for dioxin removal and related health care services in Da Nang, and has begun an environmental assessment of the Bien Hoa airbase near Ho Chi Minh City. However, the Vietnamese government and people would like to see the United States do more to remove dioxin from their country and provide help for victims of Agent Orange.

Unexploded Ordnance[59]

According to estimates, U.S. military aircraft dropped between 5 million and 7.8 million tons of ordnance on Vietnam during the war. An estimated 800,000 tons of unexploded ordnance (UXO) remain from the Vietnam War, including bombs and landmines that contaminate 20% of the

---

[56] See, for instance, Department of Defense, "Joint Press Briefing with Secretary Panetta and Vietnamese Minister of Defense Gen. Phung Quang Thanh from Hanoi, Vietnam," June 4, 2012.

[57] CQ Congressional Transcripts, "Senate Foreign Relations Committee Holds Confirmation Hearing on Various Ambassadorial and U.S. Agency for International Development Nominations," June 17, 2014.

[58] For more on the Agent Orange issue, see CRS Report RL34761, *Vietnamese Victims of Agent Orange and U.S.-Vietnam Relations*, by Michael F. Martin.

[59] This section written by Thomas Lum, CRS Specialist in Asian Affairs.

country's area and affect 5% of its arable land. There reportedly have been over 105,000 Vietnamese casualties from UXO since the end of the Vietnam War, including roughly 35,000 deaths. In 2012, there were 73 casualties. Less than 10% of UXO and landmine survivors reportedly have access to rehabilitation programs.[60]

International donors spent $8.7 million on clearance and related activities in Vietnam in 2012. The largest donors were the United States, the United Kingdom, Norway, and Germany. Between 1993 and 2012, the United States provided nearly $35.5 million for demining efforts and $26.8 million for programs for war victims.[61] In recent years, the United States has spent roughly $4.5 million annually on demining programs through the Non-proliferation, Anti-terrorism, Demining, and Related Activities (NADR) foreign assistance account.[62] Separately, since 1989, USAID's Leahy War Victims Fund has supported programs for prosthetics, physical rehabilitation, occupational training, employment, and access for the handicapped.

In December 2013, the United States and Vietnam signed a Memorandum of Understanding on cooperation to overcome the effects of "wartime bomb, mine, and unexploded ordnance" in Vietnam.[63] Unlike Laos and Cambodia, two countries heavily impacted by Vietnam War-related UXO, the Vietnamese government, through the National Mine Action Center, takes a predominant role in running and funding the country's demining efforts. In 2010, the Vietnamese government approved a five-year plan to remove UXO from up to 5,000 square kilometers (1,931 square miles) in six provinces with the help of international donors.[64]

According to some experts, more international assistance would be forthcoming if Vietnam acceded to international treaties on landmines and cluster munitions, created a civilian-led, transparent national authority on UXO, and maintained a comprehensive database.[65] Some U.S. NADR funding has been devoted to strengthening the capacity of the Vietnam Bomb and Mine Action Center, assisting Vietnam in implementing a national strategy for addressing UXO, and creating a centralized database.[66]

POW/MIA Issues

Officially, more than 1,000 Americans who served in Indochina during the Vietnam War era are still unaccounted for.[67] From 1975 through the late 1990s, obtaining a full accounting of the U.S. POW/MIA cases was one of the dominant issues in bilateral relations. Beginning in the early 1990s, cooperation between the two sides increased. By 1998, a substantial permanent U.S. staff

---

[60] Chris Brummitt, "40 Years after Vietnam Bombing, Victims Still Fall," *Associated Press*, August 14, 2013; Landmine and Cluster Munition Monitor, http://www.the-monitor.org/index.php/cp/display/region_profiles/theme/ 3160, http://www.the-monitor.org/index.php/cp/display/region_profiles/theme/3161

[61] NADR account funds.

[62] Department of State, Bureau of Political-Military Affairs, *2013 to Walk the Earth in Safety: General Information*, August 1, 2013.

[63] "Vietnam, US Sign First MOU on Bomb, Mine Clearance," *Vietnam News Brief Service*, December 17, 2013.

[64] "Vietnam Calls for International Assistance in UXO Removal," *Vietnamnet*, April 12, 2013; "Vietnam Needs $666.6M for Wartime Bomb, Mine Clearance by 2015," *Vietnam News Brief Service*, May 15, 2013.

[65] Brummett, op. cit.

[66] Department of State, *FY2012 Congressional Budget Justification for Foreign Operations*.

in Vietnam was deeply involved in frequent searches of aircraft crash sites and discussions with local Vietnamese witnesses throughout the country. The Vietnamese authorities also have allowed U.S. analysts access to numerous POW/MIA-related archives and records. The U.S. Defense Department has reciprocated by allowing Vietnamese officials access to U.S. records and maps to assist their search for Vietnamese MIAs. The increased efforts have led to account for nearly 700 missing U.S. service personnel. Hundreds of thousands of Vietnamese remain missing from the Vietnam War period. For years, Vietnam has expressed in interest in receiving U.S. help in locating and identifying the remains of these MIAs. In November 2010, the U.S. Agency for International Development (USAID) and Vietnam's Ministry of Labor and Social Affairs (MOLISA) agreed to a two-year program under which the United States was to spend $1 million to help Vietnam locate and recover the remains of the hundreds of thousands of Vietnamese soldiers missing from the Vietnam War.

Conditions in Vietnam

For the first decade after reunification in 1975, Vietnamese leaders placed a high priority on ideological purity and rigid government controls. By the mid-1980s, disastrous economic conditions and diplomatic isolation led the country to adopt a more pragmatic line, enshrined in the *doi moi* (renovation) economic reforms of 1986. Under *doi moi*, the government gave farmers greater control over what they produce, abandoned many aspects of central state planning, cut subsidies to state enterprises, reformed the price system, and opened the country to foreign direct investment (FDI). After stalling somewhat in the late 1990s, economic reforms were accelerated in the early 2000s, as Vietnam made sweeping changes that were necessary to enter the WTO. Politically and socially, the country became much less repressive, even tolerating some expressions of dissent in certain areas that had been considered sensitive. That said, although Vietnam appears to be a freer country than it was two decades ago, according to many sources human rights conditions have worsened compared to the middle of the last decade, particularly for dissenters. There are signs that factional battles among Vietnamese leaders have intensified since at least 2011. Prime Minister Nguyen Tan Dung, who has held his post since 2006, has come under increasing criticism for allegations of corruption of his allies and for an array of nationwide economic problems.

Economic Developments

During the 25 years since the *doi moi* reforms were launched, Vietnam was one of the world's fastest-growing countries. Agricultural production has soared, transforming Vietnam from a net food importer into the world's second-largest exporter of rice and the second-largest producer of coffee. The move away from a command economy also helped reduce poverty levels from around 60% in the early 1990s to less than 20% two decades later, and the government has set a goal of becoming a middle-income country by 2020.[68] A substantial portion of the country's growth has been driven by foreign investment.

---

[68] World Bank, *Taking Stock. An Update on Vietnam's Recent Economic Developments*, December 2013.

After years of annual growth rates above 7%, Vietnam's economic growth has slowed considerably following the global financial crisis of 2007. The shocks of the crisis hit Vietnam's economy hard, in part due to Vietnam's dependence on trade and on foreign direct investment inflows, and the subsequent economic difficulties increased social strife and raised concerns about the country's economic stability. Although macro-economic conditions appear to have stabilized somewhat, some of these concerns linger. In 2013, Vietnam's real GDP grew by around 5.4%, about the same level as the previous year, and its inflation rate was around 6%, significantly lower than the double-digit price increases earlier in the decade. Over the past decade, Vietnam has seen a rising income and wealth disparity, which at times has fueled discontent among Vietnam's poor and lower-income population.

Despite its considerable economic gains over the past generation, Vietnam remains a poor country; per capita GDP in 2013 was about $4,000 when measured on a purchasing power parity basis.[69] Economists point to Vietnam's failure to tackle its remaining structural economic problems—including unprofitable state-owned enterprises (SOEs), a weak banking sector, massive red tape, and bureaucratic corruption—as major impediments to continued growth. According to some sources, many if not most of Vietnam's SOEs are functionally bankrupt, and require significant government subsidies and assistance to continue operating. Although thousands of SOEs officially have been partially privatized since the early 1990s under the government's "equitization" program, most of these are small and medium-sized firms, and the government still owns substantial stakes in them. Other SOE reform measures are being discussed.[70]

Vietnam's Energy Plans[71]

As Vietnam's economy has grown, so have its energy demands, which, according to one source, grew by 15% annually in the first decade of the 2000s.[72] To help keep pace with its growing energy demand, Vietnam plans to build several nuclear power plants—and the first in Southeast Asia—in the coming decades. It is against this backdrop that Vietnam and the United States negotiated their aforementioned bilateral nuclear energy cooperation agreement. (See the "Bilateral Nuclear Energy Agreement Signed" section above.) In 2011, the Prime Minister's office published an energy plan that called for nuclear power providing around 10% of the country's electricity needs by 2030 and other projections forecast that nuclear power will provide nearly a third of the country's electricity by 2050.[73] Construction on the first plant, to be built by a Russian company in Phuoc Dinh, Ninh Thuan province, was planned to start in 2015. In January 2014, however, Vietnam's Prime Minister announced a delay until 2020, potentially pushing back the planned completion of the first reactor to the mid-2020s. Difficulties in training staff for the planned nuclear power program have been mentioned by news reports as a possible reason for the

[69] Central Intelligence Agency, *World Factbook*, May 30, 2014.

[70] For more on Vietnam's SOE sector, see CRS Report R41550, *U.S.-Vietnam Economic and Trade Relations: Issues for the 113th Congress*, by Michael F. Martin.

[71] For more on Vietnam-U.S. nuclear energy cooperation, see CRS Report R43433, *U.S.-Vietnam Nuclear Cooperation Agreement: Issues for Congress*, by Mary Beth D. Nikitin, Mark Holt, and Mark E. Manyin.

[72] Economist Intelligence Unit, *Vietnam: Energy Report*, December 16, 2009.

[73] Office of the Prime Minister, Decision No. 1208/QD-TTg, "Approval of the National Master Plan for Power Development for the 2011-2020 Period with the Vision to 2030," July 21, 2011. World Nuclear Association, "Nuclear Power in Vietnam," January 2014, http://www.world-nuclear.org/info/Country-Profiles/Countries-T-Z/Vietnam/.

delay.[74] Two additional 1,000 MWe reactors are planned to be built in nearby Vinh Hai (*Ninh Thuan 2* plant) and be brought on-line by 2026.

Vietnam's Politics and Political Structure

In general, Vietnam's experiments with political reform have lagged behind its economic changes. A new constitution promulgated in 1992, for instance, reaffirmed the central role of the VCP in politics and society, and Vietnam remains a one-party state. In practice, the Communist Party sets the general direction for policy while the details of implementation generally are left to the four lesser pillars of the Vietnamese polity: the state bureaucracy, the legislature (the National Assembly), the Vietnamese People's Army (VPA), and the officially sanctioned associations and organizations that exist under the Vietnamese Fatherland Front umbrella.

The Party's major decision-making bodies are the Central Committee, which has 175 members, and the Politburo, which has 14 members. Membership on the Politburo generally is decided based upon maintaining a rough geographic (north, south, and central) and factional (conservatives and reformers) balance. The three top leadership posts are, in order of influence, the VCP general secretary, followed by the prime minister, and the president. Since the death in 1986 of Vietnam's last "strong man," Le Duan, decision-making on major policy issues typically has been arrived at through consensus within the Politburo, a practice that often leads to protracted delays on contentious issues.

Vietnam's Leadership Team

In mid-January 2011, the ruling Vietnamese Communist Party (VCP) held a weeklong National Congress, the 11th since the Party was founded. Party Congresses, held every five years, are often occasions for major leadership realignments and set the direction for Vietnam's economic, diplomatic, and social policies.

At the 11th Party Congress, delegates selected Nguyen Phu Trong (born 1944), formerly the chairman of Vietnam's National Assembly, to serve as the next VCP General Secretary, Vietnam's top post. Prime Minister Nguyen Tan Dung (b. 1949, pronounced "dzung") retained his membership in the 14-member Politburo, and was reappointed to his post by the National Assembly later in 2011. Likewise, the Assembly approved the Party Congress's decision to select Truong Tan Sang (b. 1949) as Vietnam's next president.[75] Dung and Sang are both believed to have sought to become general secretary. Despite his apparent re-appointment, Dung's power base is believed to have been reduced at the Congress. Trong and Sang are both believed to be assertive rivals and according to some analysts battles between them have hamstrung Vietnamese policymaking.[76]

---

[74] NucNet, "PM Says Vietnam Might Delay Construction of First Nuclear Plant," January 16, 2014.

[75] The former president and VCP general secretary had both served two, five-year terms, and—in keeping with recent tradition—had stepped down for age and health reasons.

[76] Jonathan London, "South China Sea Crisis Demands Vietnam's Leadership Breakthrough," Center for Strategic and International Studies CogitAsia Blog, May 19, 2014.

The National Assembly[77]

Over the past 10-15 years, Vietnam's legislative organ, the National Assembly, has slowly and subtly increased its influence to the point where it is no longer a rubber stamp. In recent years the Assembly has vetoed Cabinet appointments, forced the government to revise major commercial legislation, and successfully demanded an increase in its powers. These include the right to review each line of the government's budget, the right to hold no-confidence votes against the government, and the right to dismiss the president and prime minister (though not the VCP general secretary).

It remains to be seen how much influence the Assembly will ultimately have over policymaking, given the VCP's dominant role and the centralization of decision-making in Vietnam. More than 85% of parliamentarians are Party members, and the VCP carefully screens all candidates before elections are held. Moreover, the Communist Party and the central government generally have *encouraged* the National Assembly's evolution into a more robust body, to help create the legal system and culture most Vietnamese leaders feel are necessary to support a modern, middle-income state. The latest elections for National Assembly members were held in May 2011.

Vietnam-China Relations

History

Vietnam's relations with China, Vietnam's most important bilateral relationship, have been fraught with ambivalence for thousands of years. China ruled Vietnam for over 1,000 years until Vietnam successfully fought for its independence in the year 939. During China's Ming dynasty (1368-1644), China ruled Vietnam from 1407 to 1428, until another rebellion drove the Chinese out. Despite this restoration of Vietnam's independence, Ming China continued to exert a profound influence on Vietnamese culture and governance, particularly among the elite.

In the 20th Century, for nearly 25 years after China's Communists defeated Chinese Nationalist forces in 1949, Beijing was an important patron for Vietnamese communists who fought first against French colonial rule and then against South Vietnam and the United States. Long-repressed Sino-Vietnamese tensions resurfaced in the 1970s, coinciding with the United States' military withdrawal from Vietnam in 1973 and communist North Vietnam's defeat of the U.S.-backed Republic of Vietnam in 1975. Beijing and Hanoi clashed over competing territorial claims, and China sought to limit Vietnamese influence in Cambodia, which also had territorial disputes with Vietnam. The turning point came in late 1978. In November of that year Vietnam formed an alliance with the Soviet Union, which had emerged as China's number one threat. The following month, Vietnam invaded Cambodia, partly in response to the communist Cambodian government's incursions into Vietnamese territory. In early 1979, China attacked Vietnam for a two month period, in a brief but bloody border conflict, during which the two sides severed relations. Vietnamese forces exacted an unexpected heavy toll on Chinese troops. Military skirmishes continued during the 1980s. In the 1990s the two sides restored relations, which have expanded greatly over the past quarter century.

---

[77] Former CRS Research Associate Lam Van Phan contributed to this section.

Relations Today

In recent years, Sino-Vietnam relations have followed seemingly contradictory trends. On the one hand, since Vietnam and China repaired relations in the early 1990s, China has become Vietnam's most important bilateral partner and its biggest trading partner. Maintaining stability and friendship with its northern neighbor is critical for Vietnam's economic development and security, and Hanoi does not undertake large-scale diplomatic moves without first calculating Beijing's likely reaction. Over the past four years, Hanoi and Beijing have continued to expand their diplomatic and party-to-party ties and appear to be seeking ways to prevent their maritime disputes from spilling over into other areas of the relationship. Many Vietnamese, particularly in the VCP, see China's Communist Party as an ideological bedfellow, as well as a role model for a country that seeks to allow more market forces into its economy without threatening the Communist Party's dominance. China also is Vietnam's largest trading partner.

On the other hand, Vietnam's historical ambivalence and suspicions of China have increased in recent years due to concerns that China's expanding influence in Southeast Asia is having a negative effect on Vietnam. These concerns, in turn, have led Vietnamese leaders to take steps to lessen their dependence on and vulnerabilities to Chinese influence. For instance, since the late 2000s Vietnam has sought to upgrade its relations with outside powers, such as the United States and Japan. In other moves widely interpreted as related to increased maritime tensions, Vietnam in 2009 signed contracts to purchase billions of dollars of new military equipment from Russia, including six Kilo-class submarines that reportedly have begun to arrive in Vietnam. According to Vietnam's most recent Defense Ministry White paper, released in 2009, Vietnam's defense budget increased by nearly 70% between 2005 and 2008.[78]

That said, Hanoi feels like it must tiptoe carefully along the tightrope between Washington and Beijing, such that improved relations with one capital not be perceived as a threat to the other. Vietnamese leaders have become increasingly sensitive to rising domestic criticism that they are being overly solicitous toward China. Vietnam's trade deficit with China has soared over the past decade, which sometimes causes bilateral trade friction; Chinese imports represent around a quarter of Vietnam's total imports by value, up from less than 10% in 2000.

The Environment

Rapid industrialization, agricultural development, and urbanization have brought an array of environmental challenges. As Vietnam's Environment Administration (VEA), which is part of the Ministry of Natural Resources and the Environment (MONRE), writes on its website, "apparently, environmental pollution and economic development is a paradoxical development of the country."[79] Among the problems that the VEA and outside observers cite are water pollution, inadequate sewage treatment facilities, deforestation, overuse of pesticides, and destruction of natural coastal and riverine features such as mangrove forests. Vietnam has a number of environmental laws and regulations, such as the 2005 Environmental Protection Law, but enforcement is frequently identified as a problem. Compounding the challenges is Vietnam's historic vulnerability to storms and flooding, particularly along the low-lying central coastal

---

[78] Vietnam, Ministry of Defense, *White Paper*, 2009, p. 38.

[79] Vietnam Environment Administration, "The Current Situation of Environment Pollution in Viet Nam," October 6, 2013.

region. The government estimates that asset losses due to natural disasters subtract around 1.5% of GDP annually, with nearly three-quarters of the losses occurring in the central provinces.[80]

It is not clear to what extent the Vietnamese government has reconciled the tension between its environmental challenges and its overriding domestic goal of becoming a middle-income economy by 2020. *Doi moi*'s emphasis on growth and output often has created a disincentive for officials and factory managers to comply with environmental regulations, as many have learned that they likely will not be punished for polluting if they increase production.

In climate modeling exercises, Vietnam often is listed as one of the most vulnerable countries to the possible effects of climate change. This is due to its climate, long coastline, and topography (particularly the extent of its low-lying, populated coastal areas), among other factors. Rising sea levels and increased precipitation associated with a warming climate are anticipated to combine with other phenomena (e.g., sinking river deltas associated with groundwater withdrawal, floodplain engineering, and sediment trapped by dams) to exacerbate problems such as salt-water intrusion and flooding; these impacts may particularly affect Vietnam's poorer communities. Additionally, Vietnam's rapid economic growth has led to increased energy demand and greenhouse gas emissions. According to one source, Vietnam's carbon dioxide emissions from fossil fuel consumption doubled between 2002 and 2011, and the government is exploring a number of options to reduce its emissions.[81]

Environmental cooperation is one of several areas targeted for expansion in the U.S.-Vietnam "comprehensive partnership." According to information provided by the State Department, the United States spent over $35 million between 2009 and early 2014 on environmental programs in Vietnam.[82] Nearly all of these funds were spent on climate change issues. In December 2013, Secretary of State Kerry in Hanoi announced that USAID would launch a Vietnam Forest and Deltas Program, under which around $25 million will be spent to help four provinces in Vietnam's Mekong delta region adapt to climate change and restore the region's "natural ecosystems." The project also is designed to help Vietnam develop and implement its national level climate change policies.[83] It is unclear to what extent these funds represent new monies, a repackaging of existing programs, or a combination of the two.

Selected Legislation in the 113th Congress

H.R. 772 (Faleomavaega). States that the United States has an interest in ensuring that "no party threatens or uses force or coercion unilaterally to assert maritime territorial claims in East Asia and Southeast Asia, including in the South China Sea.... " Condemns Chinese vessels' "use of threats or force" in the South China Sea and the East China Sea. Supports U.S. military

---

[80] Vietnam Environment Administration, "The Current Situation of Environment Pollution in Viet Nam," October 6, 2013.

[81] Energy Information Agency, *Overview Data for Vietnam*, May 30, 2013. According to the EIA, Vietnam's CO_2 emissions were around 112 million metric tons in 2011, compared to nearly 5.5 billion metric tons emitted by the United States, which has a population roughly 3.3 times as large as Vietnam's.

[82] May 5, 2014, e-mail correspondence between CRS and State Department official.

[83] State Department, "Remarks on Climate Change and the Environment," Remarks by Secretary of State John Kerry, Kien Vang Market Pier, Mekong Delta, Vietnam, December 15, 2013; USAID Press Release, "U.S.-Vietnam Project to Address Climate Change in Vietnam's Forests and Deltas," Thursday, January 16, 2014.

operations to uphold freedom of navigation rights in the waters and air space of the South China Sea and East China Sea. Requires the Secretary of State to submit to Congress a report on the negotiations over a Code of Conduct in the South China Sea. Introduced February 15, 2013; referred to House Subcommittee on Asia and the Pacific.

H.R. 1682 (Lofgren). Adds Vietnam to the li   st of countries ineligible for participating in the Generalized System of Preferences program unless the President certifies that Vietnam is meeting certain requirements in human rights and combating human trafficking. Contains a presidential waiver provision. Introduced April 23, 2013; referred to House Ways and Means Committee.

H.R. 1897 (Smith)/S. 1649 (Boozman). Vietnam Human Rights Act of 2013. Prohibits increases in many forms of U.S. non-humanitarian assistance to Vietnam over FY2012 amounts unless (a) Vietnam's human rights conditions are certified as improving, or (b) the President issues a waiver. States that the sense of Congress is that the United States should not reduce Vietnamese language services of the Voice of America and Radio Free Asia; that Vietnam should be redesignated as a country of particular concern for religious freedom; and that Vietnam's activities to combat human trafficking are insufficient to justify its elevation to "Tier 2" status in the State Department's annual trafficking in persons report. Requires the Secretary of State to submit an annual report to Congress on various matters. H.R. 1897 was introduced May 8, 2013; passed by the House 405-3 (Roll Call 435) on August 1, 2013; referred to Senate Foreign Relations Committee. S. 1649 was introduced November 5, 2013; referred to Senate Foreign Relations Committee.

H.R. 2519 (Lee). Directs the Departments of State and Veterans Affairs to provide assistance and support research to help "covered individuals" affected by Agent Orange. Defines "covered individual" as a Vietnam resident who is affected by health issues related to Agent Orange exposure between January 1, 1961, and May 7, 1975, or who lives or had lived in or near geographic areas in Vietnam that continue to contain high levels of Agent Orange, or who is affected by such health issues as the child or descendant of such resident. Introduced June 26, 2013; referred to House Subcommittee on Disability Assistance and Memorial Affairs.

H.R. 4495 (Forbes). The Asia-Pacific Region Priority Act. Contains a number of provisions regarding maritime disputes in the South China Sea and various countries' actions there. States that the United States has an interest in "maintaining freedom of navigation, freedom of the seas, respect for international law, and unimpeded lawful commerce" in the South China Sea. States that U.S. policy urges all parties to the disputes to "refrain from engaging in destabilizing activities." Introduced April 28, 2014; referred to House Armed Services Committee and House Foreign Affairs Subcommittee on Asia and the Pacific.

H.R. 4254 (Royce). Imposes financial and immigration sanctions on certain Vietnamese who are complicit in human rights abuses. Requires the President to submit to Congress a list of individuals complicit in certain human rights abuses. Introduced March 14, 2014; referred to the House Foreign Affairs Committee, Ways and Means Committee, Financial Services Committee, and Judiciary Subcommittee on Immigration and Border Security.

H.J.Res. 116 (Kinzinger)/S.J.Res. 39 (Reid). State that Congress approves of the U.S.-Vietnam nuclear cooperation agreement. H.J.Res. 116 introduced June 9, 2014; referred to House Committee on Foreign Affairs. S.J.Res. 39 introduced June 9, 2014; referred to Senate Foreign Affairs Committee.

H.Res. 218 (Royce). "Encourages" the State Department to redesignate Vietnam as a country of particular concern for "particularly severe violations of religious freedom." "Urges" the State Department to demonstrate that the expansion of U.S.-Vietnam relations will depend on improvements in religious freedom in Vietnam. Introduced May 16, 2013; referred to the House Subcommittee on Asia and the Pacific.

S. 929 (Cornyn). The Vietnam Human Rights Sanctions Act. Requires the President to (a) compile and submit to Congress a list of Vietnamese deemed to be complicit in human rights abuses, (b) prohibit these individuals from entering the United States, and (c) impose financial sanctions on these individuals. Authorizes the President to waive sanctions to comply with international agreements or if in the U.S. national interest. Expresses the sense of Congress that the Secretary of State should designate Vietnam as a country of particular concern (CPC) with respect to religious freedom, and that bilateral relations cannot expand unless Vietnam's human rights conditions improve. Introduced May 9, 2013; referred to the Senate Committee on Foreign Relations.

S.J.Res. 36 (Menendez). States that Congress favors the U.S.-Vietnam nuclear cooperation agreement. Except for certain allied countries and institutions, prohibits issuance of any export license pursuant to a nuclear cooperation agreement 30 years after the agreement's entry into force. Introduced May 22, 2014; referred to Senate Foreign Relations Committee.

S.Res. 167 (Menendez). States that the United States has an interest in freedom of navigation and overflight in Asia-Pacific maritime domains. "Condemns" maritime vessels' and aircrafts' use of coercion, threats, or force in the South China Sea and East China Sea to assert disputed maritime or territorial claims or alter the status quo. "Supports" ASEAN and China's efforts to develop a Code of Conduct for the South China Sea. "Supports" U.S. military operations in the Western Pacific, including in partnership with other countries, to support the freedom of navigation. Introduced June 10, 2013; passed by the Senate by unanimous consent July 29, 2013.

Figure 1. Map of Vietnam

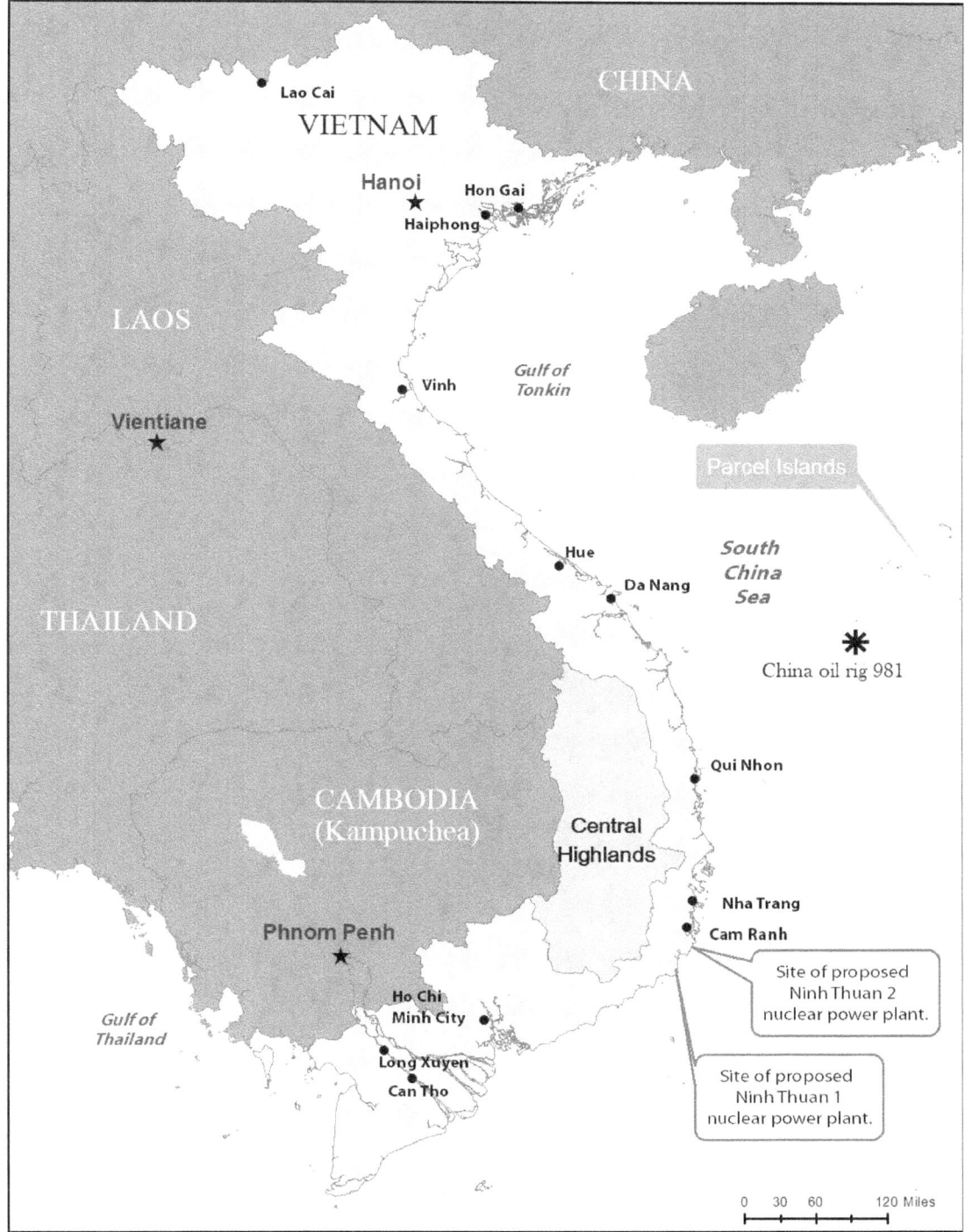

Source: CRS.

Author Contact Information

Mark E. Manyin
Specialist in Asian Affairs
mmanyin@crs.loc.gov, 7-7653